Adam and Eve

Om KIDZ
An imprint of Om Books International

Along time ago, when God made the Heaven and the Earth, He was very pleased. Different animals walked on land, birds flew freely in the sky, and there were fish swimming in the blue waters. God said, "Now I shall make human beings to look after all of them".

So, God made Adam, the first man, from dust. He gave him a beautiful garden, called Eden, to live in. But, Adam was alone. God looked at him and thought, "It would be nice for him to have someone to be with. I shall give him a friend." So God made the first woman from Adam's rib. She was called Eve.

The Garden of Eden, where Adam and Eve lived, was beautiful. It was lush with vegetation and wildlife. There were delicious fruits to eat and a river of cool, fresh water to drink from.

There were two special trees in Eden. One was called the tree of life, and the other was known as the tree of knowledge of good and evil. God said, "You may eat fruit from all the other trees in the garden, but you must not eat from the tree of knowledge of good and evil. If you do so, you will die."

God then blessed Adam and Eve. He said, "You will have children, and all of you must take good care of the earth. Keep it as beautiful as I have given it to you."

Time passed. Adam and Eve looked after the garden with love. All the creatures lived well and they were very, very happy. It was just as God wished. However, one day Satan, the Devil, entered Eden slyly and disguised himself as a snake. He then went up to Eve and asked, "Did God say that we may eat any fruit from any tree?"

Eve replied, "We may eat from any tree except that one in the middle of the garden. If we eat from that tree we will die."

The snake whispered, "That is not true. Do you know why God does not want us to eat from the tree of knowledge? It is because if we do so, we will know about good and evil and become as wise as He is."

The snake's cunning words made Eve think. She looked at the tree. The fruit looked delicious. "It would be nice to be wise!" she said and picked a fruit, and took a bite. When she went to Adam with fruit, Adam was horrified and refused to take a bite. But as he loved Eve and became curious about good and evil, he eventually ate it too. Suddenly, they started feeling different. They realised that they had no clothes on and became ashamed. They covered themselves with leaves.

When God came to the Garden next time, he found them hiding themselves. God asked them why they were ashamed. Slowly, they came out and told Him how they now felt. God understood. "Did you eat from the Tree of Knowledge?", He asked.

They admitted their disobedience. Adam blamed Eve. He said, "She made me eat it." Eve said it was not her fault, "It was the snake's trick."

God was not happy. He said that they would have to bear the punishment for their disobedience. He also said, "You will from now on lead a difficult life and one day you will have to die."

God then gave them clothes made of animal skin and turned them out of the Garden of Eden.